EVERYDAY IS MOTHER'S DAY

BY K. L. JOYNER

Everyday is Mother's Day is a book of poems
Dedicated to the beautiful mothers of the world
Past and present.

TO MOM,
The greatest blessing in my life
Has always been having you in it.

TABLE OF CONTENTS

1.......EVERYDAY IS MOTHER'S DAY
2.......MY MOTHER
3.......BLESSED BE THE ONE CALLED MOTHER
4.......A MOTHER'S SONG
5.......MOM'S BOY
6.......MOM & GOD
7.......IT'S GETTING LATE
8.......RED ROSE OR WHITE
9.......SMALL THINGS
10......LISTEN TO MOTHER
11......EVERY DAY MOTHERS
12......THANK GOD
13......MY MOM
14......MOTHER'S SACRIFICE
15......MOTHER DEAREST
16......SIPPING COFFEE WITH MOM
17......MOTHERS AND DAUGHTERS
18......MY ANGEL
19......A MOTHER'S LIFE
20......MOTHER'S HUG
21......THE HEART OF A WOMAN
22......LESSONS FROM MOTHER
23......HIP, HIP, HOORAY FOR MOTHER'S DAY
24......REMEMBERING MOTHER
25......A PRAYING MOTHER
26......I WONDER
27......QUEEN'S MOVE
28......MOTHER'S DAY IS MOTHER'S DAY
29......WHY MOTHER'S DAY
30......MOTHER'S BABY

TABLE OF CONTENTS

31......LOVE YOUR MOTHER
32......MOTHER'S WORRY
33......MOTHER'S SMILE
34......MOTHER TOLD ME
35......A MOTHER'S LOVE
36......MOTHER TO MOTHER
37......TOO SOON
38......TOMORROW, TOMORROW
39......A SON'S PRAYER
40......A MOTHER'S PRAYER

EVERYDAY IS MOTHER'S DAY

Dear, Sweet, Precious, Mother
There never has been
And there never will be
Another.

Only the love of God
Can compare,
To the love you give,
It's that rare.

I am grown now,
No longer the child.
There's no need for you to cuddle me
After I've fallen.

No need for you to watch me with the eyes of a hawk,
As I refuse to crawl and struggle with my first steps.
No more packing my lunch for school,
No more refusing to let me play,
Until I've finished my homework.
Yes, I still remember the rule.

All of those times have come and passed,
But in my memory, they will forever last.
How could any forget the love of thy Mother?
This petty day they give you,
It could never begin to compare
To the compassion you show
And the love you display, every minute of every day.

Not one!
But everyday, should be Mother's Day
And I pray that in Heaven,
It is that way.

MY MOTHER

I owe you everything,
Life, Love, Devotion, Strength.
You taught me all,
And made me think.

Never was there a day
That I didn't feel love.
Never was there a thing,
We didn't rise above.

In poverty, we lived.
But I never knew,
And that was all thanks to you.

You shelled out love
Like raindrops fall,
And gave out discipline
When we thought we knew it all.

Never will there be another
Who'll have more effect on my life.

Thank you, Mother,
For your sacrifice.

BLESSED BE THE ONE CALLED MOTHER

Mother!
Just the mention of your name on my lips
Should make my heart rend.

And my eyes,
Spill, sweet or bitter waters.
Each in according to thou sorrow
Or thy gladness.

There will never be another
More precious than your Mother.
No earthly treasure more rich,
No ivory or gold,
More pure.

Time can never diminish your place in my heart.
Nor death make me forget your warm embrace.
For in you is love, and it transcends all.
It's power given by the Most High,
God, Himself.

Mother!
Great Mother!
Gateway to the world,
Creator of life.

You are Heaven's reward on Earth,
You are the treasure amongst treasures.
The gift amongst gifts.

And yes, I cry tears of joy
Whenever your precious name
Crosses my lips.

A MOTHER'S SONG

When I first heard her voice I couldn't speak,
I was lying in my cradle as she sang me to sleep.

Later the melody changed, but the song was always the same.
Even when she said, clean your room or make your bed.
Her angelic voice sang in my head.

A mother's song may start as a tune,
But its legacy is love
And that, even time can't consume.

Her music echoes in our ears
And even long after she's gone
Her tune will play, On and on.
Evoking in us laughter, and sometimes, even tears
And when we hear them, we'll feel
She's always near.
Still watching over us, still singing.

That's the power of a mother's song.
We are her music,
And as long as we're here.
How can she ever be gone?

Mothers of the world
We hear you in Heaven,
We hear you on Earth.

Your music,
It's Clear, Loud, and Strong.

For God made you the instrument
Life's story is played on.

MOM'S BOY

Streetlight Kenneth was my name
And my brother Jerome was called the same.
When that street light came on,
We were gone.

Heading straight to the house,
Faster than a mouse.
It was Mother's Rule,
And Mother Ruled.

I never thought about it
As a kid.
When she spoke, that's what I did.

I didn't realize,
That she was helping me
To live.

Now I'm older and I can see,
What my mother had always seen.

That those who play in the dark,
Sometimes, never make it back
To the Light.

MOM & GOD

Debra burn the rice again
But momma doesn't care.

Not today, It's God's Day again
And she's going to church
To see her friend.

Mom and God have been partners for years,
That's why she has no fears
Or any tears.

When it comes to His Word,
She's sincere, and He's all ears.

There's nothing she asks, He won't do
I mean cancer three times,
And He saw her through.

She's still driving at eighty-two.
What would you do,
If God was looking out, like that for you?

That's why on Sundays,
I don't stray.

Because I want Him to lookout for me,
In that same way.

IT'S GETTING LATE

Don't wait too late,
Even mothers have a date.
A time when she and God will have a talk,
A time when she and God will take a walk.

So don't hold back anything,
Because one day you will be willing
To give up anything.

For just one more moment of her time,
But you'll be too late.
She had a date.

Now she's dining in the Heavens above,
Surrounded by all those she loves.

So before it's too late,
Tell her, "Mother I Love You!
Mother, no one in this world
Is above you."

Because every mother has a date,
And Our Father In Heaven,
IS NEVER LATE.

RED ROSE OR WHITE

It was a beautiful Mother's Day
And I was in Savannah.
Enjoying River Street,
Without a care in the world.

I had gotten Mom a bear and candy
And was going to drop them off
On my way home.

When a lady walked up to me
With a basket of flowers
And asked, "Red Rose or White?"

For a moment the words
Meant nothing to me.
Then suddenly, they meant everything.

I looked at this woman,
With just those four words,
She had reminded me of everything,
That I needed to be thankful for.

I said, "Red please."
Then I hurried to my Mother's house.

SMALL THINGS

A Mother's gift to a child
Could be as simple as a smile,
Or a piece of candy before dinner time.

Little things that shouldn't
Mean anything.
But meant everything
To a boy of five.

I've carried those moments of love
She shared with me
All of my life.

They have made me, Kinder
And stronger, but mostly.

A Son who still
Loves His Mother
Very, Very, Much.

HAPPY MOTHER'S DAY
To every Kind Mother
In the World.

LISTEN TO MOTHER

When a mother cries
It's said, even the angels are sad
And depending on her tears
The angels are mad.
The connection between Heaven and Women
Will never be seen by a man.
How could it be?
Only they and God
Share the power of life.

It gives her sight and understanding
Beyond her years.
That sometimes brings the tears
Because the death of a child
Will drive that mother wild.

Because she saw it, before it came to be
That's why she cries, even though she knew,
There was nothing she could do.

That's why mothers never rest,
To busy preparing their children for every test.

Instilling in them, Both, Love, and God.
Because she knows, this world can be hard,
And, So, Very, Very, Cold.

EVERY DAY MOTHERS

It's still dark outside,
Not a sound in the house.
Then suddenly, there's movement
Only quiet, like a mouse.

It's a routine that's been done
For years.

With the stealth of a cat,
She moves away from the covers.
Letting her man get one more hour of rest,
Because, when it comes to being a wife
She's the best.

Now into the kitchen, breakfast time
She's always the first one at work,
And the last one to leave.

No holiday pay, no weekends off.
Even though, when it comes to this house
She's the boss.

She knows she picked the life
Of a mother and a wife,
And it requires
A never-ending sacrifice.

And will continue to do so,
For the rest of her life.

And she will gladly do it,
Without thinking twice.

THANK GOD

God was kind to me,
When I first came to this world.

I wanted to be a Boy
And not a Girl.

I wanted to be with someone
Who would love me true.

And low and behold, Mother.
He gave me to You.

MY MOM

Just looking at my mother
Makes me smile.
So proud I am, of all she is
And all she has been.

She's been to Heaven and Hell
And back again.
And done it mostly,
For Family, and Friends.

There's no lock she can't break
You know, the ones built around
Mostly hate.

I really believe Saint Peter's
Got a job waiting for her
At the Pearly Gates.

In the meantime,
She's still helping all of the family to get in,
Before it's too late.

Before She and God
Have that date.

MOTHER'S SACRIFICE

Let me tell you of a life,
That's filled with constant sacrifice.

Of someone who's willing
To slide down the jagged edge of a knife.

Who would fight off Satan in Hell
With only a bat, if it came to that
Anything to keep her family intact.

That's the power of a Mother
And on Earth, there is no other.

None, that would risk it all for you.
None, who would take the fall for you.

Mothers have lived in Hell for years,
So their babies could grow up with no fears.

Some gave up their youth,
Others gave up their life.

Only a Mother would make that sacrifice.

MOTHER DEAREST

Mother dearest,
So rarely are you truly appreciated.
Yes, we love you
And yes, we need you.

You hold everything in your hands.
The power in your man, begins with his belief
In you.

Without it, he's nothing
Can do, nothing.
Will become, nothing.

Your compassion is your strength,
Your love is your power.

With it, you make us believe
Anything and Everything, is possible.

The loss of you, is the loss
Of all that we hold dear.

So, to any who still have their Mother,
Know that there will never be another.

Who will ever care for you more.

SIPPING COFFEE WITH MOM

As the years go by
And my mom gets older.
I realize I'm getting
Older too.

Usually, we sip coffee
In the mornings and talk.
These times have become golden to me.

I treat everyone,
Like it's our last one together,
Because it could be.

God has blessed her
With a long and healthy life.

Yes, there have been battles
But He has made her a campaigner.

Armored up and battle-weary,
Still, she hasn't relinquished her sword
And thanks to her, I've picked mine up.

So now, we sip coffee in the mornings
And still, fight the good fight.

I wonder if Heaven's
Got creamer.

MOTHERS AND DAUGHTERS

Mothers love their sons
But having a daughter
Sets things in order.

She follows mom step for step
Little, little hands
Trying to do more than she thinks,
She can.

Mom just smiles inside,
All that girl power
Bursting with pride.

She'll coach her through pampers,
She'll be patient with the first steps
And once those first words are spoken
God only knows, what will happen next.

Preteen years are the best,
Because Mothers and teenage Daughter's
Now that's a test.
But in the end, Mothers always win.

Because good Mothers and Daughters
Are the best of friends,
And will remain so,
Until, the very End.

MY ANGEL

When I was young
I lived with a fright.
I would cry uncontrollably,
Matters not, day or night.

Just when all hope seemed to be gone
An angel would come in,
Swooping me up into her arms,
Singing gently into my ears,
Making all of my worries disappear.

She easily wiped away, all my tears
And at the same time, all of my fears.

Finally, I've learned what's going on,
I've even learned her name.

I call her, Mom.

A MOTHER'S LIFE

A mother's life is never her own,
Too many problems, too many things
Going on.

She must be loving to her husband
And nurturing to her children.
Balancing her family, while staying
In everyone's ears.

Reminding him of how strong he is,
And them, of how much she loves them.
Always reaffirming to everyone else, their worth
But no one comforts her, no one understands.

That's the power of a woman,
She gives and gives, so that others may live.
For once we should all thank her,
Hug her around her neck, kiss her face, and pray.

Thank the Lord in the Heavens above,
For sending you a Mother
Who was filled with Love.

MOTHER'S HUG

When I think about Mother's Day
I think of a five-year-old
With a quarter.

Going up aisle after aisle,
Looking for a thingamajig
Or a whatchamacallit.
Anything, as long as I had a present
For mom.

Then I was eleven, two dollars this time.
Enough for a card and a bear.
My smile was ridiculous,
As I gave them to her.

And that hug, oh my God!
There has never been anything
More powerful than my Mother's Hugs.

She'd wrapped her arms around me,
Like an angel would,
And as long as she holds you,
You're in Heaven.

I'm no longer a child, but I still go up
Aisle after aisle.
Looking for that thingamajig,
Or whatchamacallit.

But mostly, I'm waiting
Waiting for Mother's Day,
Waiting for that hug.

THE HEART OF A WOMAN

The heart of a woman
Is filled with layers,
And those layers, come with many
Players.

Those who play a small or large part,
In the weakening or the strengthening
Of that heart.

Her children automatically get through.
What else is the heart to do?
They came from her womb,
So they're one in the same.

Children are simply, their Mothers,
With different names.

Now a husband can't make that claim,
He must continuously work,
Sometimes in vain.

Because the heart might choose to forget his name,
And their relationship will never,
Be the same.

So husbands work constantly,
At keeping that spark.
The heat from his love warms her heart.

Be the best man that you can be, at all times
And if you truly play your part.

Only God can separate you,
From her heart.

LESSONS FROM MOTHER

Husbands usually pick a woman,
Who reminds them of their Mother
In some small way.

Maybe in kindness, maybe in strength.
Maybe in the way, she makes him think.

Matters not,
If she's still here.
Or, if she's gone.

A Mother's teachings to her son,
Will live on.

She,
Would want him to have a wife,
That's Sweet, Kind, and Nice.

But mostly,
A good marriage
That's built through God.

So they'll have someone to help them,
When, and if, things get hard.

HIP HIP HOORAY FOR MOTHER'S DAY

Hip, hip, hooray
Hip, hip, hooray

Another Mother's Day is on the way,
Another chance for us, to speak or say.
Words of love, prayers of thanks.

We know, we never do or say enough
For what you've done for all of us.

Those who had a true mother, truly understand
No matter, how long, or short
Her time was spent with us,
Here on Earth.

Her love remains, locked in our hearts
And even with the coming of Death itself,
Still, it will not part.

Like all real love, it transcends plains
And one day in Heaven,
Will reunite again.

So,
Hip, hip hooray
Hip, hip hooray
Mother's Day is on the way.

REMEMBERING MOTHER

Remembering Mother on Mother's Day,
It's not even an easy thing to say.
To live through it, through her passing.
Now that's a moment, that's forever lasting.

Time slowed down to a complete stop,
There is no more movement between the tick,
And the tock.

You try to remember everything you ever did together,
You even try to make God change the weather.
She so loved the pretty days in the sun,
She'd hate to leave in the rain,
Just thinking about it, just adds more pain.

If it wasn't for God
On days like this,
Most of us would go insane.
It' He who gets us through,
Most of the pain.

By letting us know, we'll see her again,
That's my understanding, that's my belief.

There are those who handle lost in a different way,
Mine is to trust God, Believe in Him
And pray.

And that's exactly what I'll do
When my Mother is no longer here
On Mother's Day.

A PRAYING MOTHER

I've had a praying mother,
Most of my life.
She's prayed for me and my siblings,
But for me the most.

I'm the one who really got lost,
I'm the one who really strayed,
And for me, my mother really prayed.

God answered her prayer, much to my despair.
He stopped me cold, in my tracks
And made me understand,
There was no going back.

It was either, on to God
Or, on to glory.
There was no other offer,
 End of story.

Nowadays, I'm the one who lives to pray
Or, speak to God, should I say?
On most days, it's for an extension of life
But not for me, I ask for Mother.

Who's slowly approaching the end of her life,
I pray He'll let her live it twice.

She just looked at me, and said, "That's nice.
But Jesus has already made that sacrifice."

I WONDER

I saw a picture of my Mother and Father,
Sitting together on a couch.
She was twenty and he was twenty-four.
Her beauty was something that you couldn't ignore.

I've never even thought of my Mother's face,
In any way, other than, that's mom.
But as an old man now, myself
I can see that my mother was a beautiful woman.

I'd never really thought of her life,
Before our life together.
She had put her life on stop,
To take care of us kids and pop's.

Giving up so much of herself,
Her days, her weeks, her years.
My mom is a woman of eighty-two now,
My Father, seventeen years, gone to glory.

Sometimes I wonder, what she wonders
I pray, that she is as happy with her life,
As we are, with her being in our lives.

Because,
She is not only the best Mother I know,
But also, She's the Best Person.

QUEEN'S MOVE

The true measure of a happy life,
Starts with the family,
And that begins with the husband
And wife.

You would think,
The man calls the shots,
But no shot will ever be fired.
If that woman has no desire,
To be fired upon.
Only she can put the bullets in his gun.

Just like in the game of chess,
The Queen is the most powerful piece,
On the board.

In life, a Mother's movements
Are the same.

A Mother moves all over her world,
Protecting her man and her children.
All the while advancing the family
Towards victory.

A victory that's called
A HAPPY LIFE.

MOTHER'S DAY IS MOTHER'S DAY

Mother's Day is Mother's Day,
Candy and flowers are on the way.
A bear holding a heart, with the words
I love you, sometimes
Gets a say.

The happiness we get from making her smile,
And sometimes, cry.
Brings a tear also, to our eyes.
Adding another block of wood,
To our already burning love for her.

There's no gift too costly,
Not a thing too great.
Nothing could ever compare to the love,
Mother has put on our plates.

So, make her smile
Make her cry,
Make her laugh,
Try, try, try.

Set her heart ablaze, with the happiest of thoughts
Fill it with so much love, until she can no longer walk.

Then drown her heart in a sea of love,
And when there's nothing else to say,
She'll know what we've known
Since that very first day.

That MOTHER'S DAY, IS, MOTHER'S DAY.
And simply, our love for her
Put on display.

WHY MOTHER'S DAY

A card and a bear will last for years,
But red, red, roses
Always brings her to tears.

Decisions, decisions
Of course, it will be both.

Yep, it's that time again
That day when she can't say no,
Can't refuse to be pampered,
Can't make us go.

The stars have all aligned in Heaven above,
It's her day again, it's the day of love.
The day when all the angels in Heaven hold hands,
And circle the world.

For twenty-four hours,
They sing the praises of women.
Through the windows in Heaven,
That the women of this world
Have opened, and made.

MOTHER'S DAY,
May sound nice.
But, what we're truly celebrating,
Is a women's sacrifice.

For in Heavens, She is known
AS THE BRINGER OF LIFE.

MOTHER'S BABY

I was only twelve months old,
I had no understanding of life.

Still fumbling with sounds and smells,
But I knew her face, her touch, her smell.

I didn't know love,
But I loved her so much.

I knew she was someone,
That I could trust.

LOVE YOUR MOTHER

All Mothers aren't, Sweet, Kind, or Nice
But all Mothers make an incredible sacrifice.

They risk everything,
With the bringing of a new life.
Only God can hold them to the Light,
Only He can judge whether they've been wrong,
Or, they've been right.

We see them,
But we don't have perfect sight.
We see good in the day,
But not in the night.

We can't see past fears,
And we can't see through tears.
So just trust in the love,
You have for her,
And everything will become clear.

As God brings her,
Closer and closer, to your heart..

Until you won't know
Where she ends,
And Heaven starts.

MOTHER'S WORRY

A Mother's worst,
No, her only fear.
Is that her child is gone,
And she is still here.

That's why, constantly
She prays to God.
And to her child, or children
She seems so hard.

She already knows the coldness
Of this world,
And in it, children get lost
And some children get crossed.
Sometimes, crossed, out of life itself.

So, mothers will be hard
They will seem mean.
They will run your life,
Like it's, their regime.

But, after the years have passed,
And you're still here,
Old and gray.

There will never be a moment,
When you don't remember her
Being, Sweet and Oh so Kind.

She was your vessel to love.
The creator of your life,
And for you, there was never a day
That she didn't make, a sacrifice.

MOTHER'S SMILE

When I was young,
When I was a child.
My Mother would look at me,
And simply smile.

Her smile was so bright,
That it could block out the Sun.
It made me skip, it made me run.

It was like a butterfly,
Had gotten a loose,
Inside of my heart.

But now, I'm older.
A grown man,
With a child of my own.

And now,
My child is grown.

Still, Mother is here
And I am blessed.

But now I don't need to see,
Her beautiful smile cross her lips.

For me,
Just knowing I can still see her,
And, Touch, Her, is eternal bliss.

Mother's smile is so powerful.
Mother's smile is so bright.
Every day with her is Heaven,
There are no nights.

MOTHER TOLD ME

My Mother has tried,
To prepare me for years.
She'd say," One day I'm not going to Be Here."

I'd just act like,
What she said was absurd.
But she'd stare me down,
To make sure, I'd heard, her words.

She'd lost her mother, very young
She was just a child.
Barely in her teens,
She knows what losing a Mother means.

It means, the end
Of your lifeline from God,
That was here on Earth.

I know I'll never be prepared,
So, I'm not going to even try.

I know the day She leaves this World,
Is the day the best part of me will die.

My relationship with God, is strong
So I will live on.

He's the only one,
Who can ease my pain,
And has already.

By promising me,
That I'll see her again.

A MOTHER'S LOVE

All new Mothers soon discover,
That loving their children is not enough.
You must make them strong,
You must make them tough.

In a world designed to destroy the weak,
You must make them able to compete.
But still, hold onto compassion,
And hold onto love.

It's like teaching,
The strongest man in the world,
To cradle a dove.

That's why breakfast was always hot,
And kisses and hugs were around the clock.
Tears were wiped away on the spot,
A small cut to your leg,
And she became your doc.

A Mother's Love, it's full-time.
I mean, around the clock.
No matter, where you go
Or, what you do.

A Mother's Love,
It's always, with you.

MOTHER TO MOTHER

Mother to Mother,
Be mindful of what your children see you do,
Because they will grow up emulating you.

Your Daughters will take whatever you have taken.
So accept nothing, but the love, of a good man.

Let her see the love and respect,
That her Father has for you,
And she will accept nothing less,
For herself.

Your Sons will see,
How they are suppose to treat a woman.
With Class and Understanding,
Also, Love and Respect.

They will cherish their wives,
For the rest of their lives.

Mother to Mother,
Make no mistake.
Getting a husband and children,
Is easy to do.

But holding it all together,
For a lifetime.
Depends on the woman,
In you.

TOO SOON

To many Mothers are not here today,
Too soon, they've been taken away.

But they will forever live in the memories,
Of the ones they've loved,
And of those, who have loved them.

So on Mother's Day, remember your Mother
It was she who brought you into this world.

They say God doesn't make mistakes,
Even, when He comes for a Mother Early.
God is God, so that's not up for debate.

My only wish is,
That when it comes to Mothers,
Going to Heaven, Early.
I pray God, finds Himself
Always, running Late.

TOMORROW, TOMORROW

When I was a kid,
I would ask my Mother,
Some of the craziest things.

Like, "Momma can I go to the moon?"
And her answer would always be the same.

She would say, "Tomorrow.
Tomorrow you can go."
But tomorrow never came.

Sixty years have gone by now,
They were right when they said,
"Time can fly."

Now,
It's Mother's time to talk crazy.
She tells me about Angels and Heaven,
And that one day she will have to go.

And I say,
"Tomorrow, tomorrow you can go."

But if it's up to me,
Tomorrow, will never come.

A SON'S PRAYER

God has blessed me,
Beyond my wildest dreams.

My Mother is still here,
Those who still have theirs,
Know exactly, what I mean.

For those whose Mothers,
Have left this world already.

She will be waiting for you,
Standing at the Gates of Heaven.
So make sure you do what's right,
Every day and every night.

That's a Mother's Love for you,
It transcends life, itself.
Not Fame, nor Wealth,
Not even your Health can compare,
Her love is that rare.

Who wouldn't give up their life today?
If it would make their Mother stay,
Another Year, Another Month
Another Week, Another Day.

I can't begin to tell you,
How many times God has heard me pray,
And my prayer is always the same.

I ask for more time,
But not for myself.
I ask for my Mother,
And no one else.

A MOTHER'S PRAYER

Lord protect my children,
From the evils of the world.

Where they are weak,
Make them strong.

Lead them into the light,
Of your protection.
Under the blanket of Your Word.
Cover them.

The sacrifice has already been made,
The cross has been carried.
The door has been opened,
For the resurrection of life.

Lord take my children by the hand,
Let them feel your power,
Let them feel your touch,
Let them feel your love,
And they will never get enough.

Lord, it's on Your Word,
That I stand.
Lord, it's on Your Word,
That I pray.

For the Souls of my children,
Protect them Lord,
Come what may.

Amen.